I0109046

# God's Got It Like That

### Poems by
### Deborah L. Hayman

## Words of Inspiration

Isaiah 50:4

The Lord GOD hath given me the tongue of the learned, that I should know how to speak a word in season to him that is weary: he wakeneth morning, by morning, he wakeneth mine ear to hear as the learned.

©2015 by Deborah L. Hayman
First Edition

All Rights Reserved

No part of this publication may be reproduced or transmitted in any form or by any means electronic or mechanical, including photocopy, recording, or any information storage and retrieval system, without permission in writing from both the copyright owner and the publisher. Please direct inquiries to:

*Deborah L. Hayman*
*Words of Inspiration Ministries*
*P.O. Box 38432*
*St. Louis, MO 63138*

ISBN: 978-1-4276-1899-3

Cover Image and Design:
*Fourthcrown Studios*

Printed in the United States of America by:
*Witty Writings Press*

Partial funding provided by the
Solomon's Temple Church Family of
St. Louis, Missouri

# Dedication

To my children—Demetrius, Jessica, Jennifer; my grandson Demetrius Jr.; my spiritual leaders—Bishop James E. Holloway, Sr., Co-Pastor Dr. Linda Holloway; and my Solomon's Temple Church family, for your timeless love and endless support. I love you all with all my heart!!

# Forward

It gives us great joy and pleasure to forward this book of poems by Minister Deborah Hayman. Minister Hayman has the impulse of God as she writes with the compassion, conviction, and nurturing of God's spirit.

We can see (energeo—energy) God's activity working in her. Truly it is God who is at work in her. It speaks of an effectual and productive energy, the infinite power of God Himself in action. ***God powers the One who energizes her spiritual progress.*** Minister Hayman perseveres because she is energized by Him. Because there is no limit to His power, we know He will ultimately complete what He has begun in her (Phil. 1:6). ***The best is yet to come.***

Surely God can and does accomplish purpose through His power at work in Minister Hayman that goes beyond her ability to plan, reason, or even dream. That inner power flows from God Himself and is the basis of her sufficiency to complete such a work. You truly will be inspired, encouraged, uplifted, motivated and blessed after reading and meditating on these poems. May God's energy continue to flow within you.

Bishop Dr. Ivory L. Bailey, Jr.

# Acknowledgements

I must first and foremost thank my almighty God and give Him all the praise that's forever due His name. Next, I would like to thank my spiritual leaders, Bishop James Holloway and Co-Pastor Linda Holloway for encouraging me with love and support to always obey and do the work of the Lord. I love you both dearly.

I would also like to thank my sister Tina, my backbone, my encourager, my strength, for always allowing me to bounce ideas off her, and helping me with even the smallest detail of this project.

To my God's Got It Like That team, for without them, this project would not have been possible at this time: MERRI J.(smile), Dashika B., Joyce W., Tina D., and Carmen T., thank you all for letting the Lord use you. I greatly appreciate Linda L., Cheryl C., Felicia H., Sharon F. and the rest of my Solomon's Temple family. Thank you all so very much for your continued support and prayers. I love and appreciate you more than you'll ever know. You're the first ones to hear the poems when God gives them to me, and just like our spiritual leaders, you encourage, encourage, encourage!! One cannot ask for a greater spiritual family. Thank you Timothy H. of Witty Press, you are truly a God-send! You are the best of the best!

To my twins, Jessica and Jennifer, thank you for your patience, love and advice as I endeavored to bring this project to completion; and for also reading and proofing my poems and scriptures with me before this book was sent to the publisher. To my twins and my son Demetrius, I thank you for always understanding how important the work of the Lord is to me. After God, you are the closest to my heart!!

Finally, count it to my head and not to my heart if I failed to mention anyone. However, I thank you for your support and encouragement in all that you've done to bring this project into completion.

# Table of Contents

*Praise the Lord!*

## God's Got It Like That

I feel like bragging this morning, my friends today
No, and it's not at all about me
But it's all about my great, big, wonderful Savior
That with the natural eye, I can't even see.

But my Lord is able to move mountains from my life
And raise me up from valleys so deep
He can cause a blind man to see, dear hearts
And a lame man to walk, and even leap.

Now, don't ask me how He does it
For He can even make a wall fall down flat
But I can tell you this about our Lord today
God's got it like that.

God's got it like that
Oh, you don't know what I'm talking about
How much time do you have this morning
To look at a few battles He has already fought.

Yes, God's got it like that
From a fiery furnace, He delivered three
And out of nothing, the world we live in
Our Savior caused it to be.

Oh, God's got it like that
He can close a hungry lion's mouth
And rain, He can make fall, refreshing us all
When we are in a drought.

Our Lord can heal the broken hearted
And speak peace in the midst of a storm
He can also call angels to encamp around us
So that the devil can do us no harm.

Oh yes, our God is the great I AM
He's whoever you need Him to be
Do you need healing, delivering, or to be made whole
Or do you need to be made free?

For God's got it like that
So do I need to say more
Because just thinking about all He's done for me
Makes me want to hit the floor.

And praise our wonderful Savior, this morning
For from out of darkness, opening my eyes
And letting me see, it's from Him and Him only
Is where my total help lies.

Oh, I could go on and on my friends today
But talking about Him makes me want to shout
Because there have been times He even answered
before I called
Now that's what I'm talking about.

And what's so good about our Lord today
Is He's able to meet us no matter where we're at
Now I can't tell you how He can help you, you, and me
at the same time
But you see God's got it like that!

## SCRIPTURE REFERENCE
*Joshua 6:20*
*Daniel 6:16-22*
*St. Matthew 17:20*
*Ephesians 3:20*

## A Breakthrough Is Coming, And It Has Your Name On It

I'm excited on this morning
Yes, I just want to praise my blessed Lord
Because God showed me something as I was praying
About a situation that seemed so hard.

For the longest He said, hold on my child
I'm going to do it, so don't let go
Keep doing what I tell you to do
For your deliverance, it is so.

But now the tides have turned, my friends today
No, on this news I cannot sit
For God said, a breakthrough is coming
And it has your name on it.

Oh, a breakthrough is coming, and it has your name on it
People give me some shouting room
For when God spoke it in my spirit
He let me know that my blessing is soon.

Yes, a breakthrough is coming, and it has your name on it
No, my waiting, it wasn't in vain
For the Lord showed me, for my troubles
He's going to pour down a deliverance rain.

A breakthrough is coming and it has your name on it
Oh excuse me, if you will
For I'm trying to keep it together
But my soul is revved up, it's filled.

For you see, through God I've blessed others,
and they received their blessings
Though my deliverance seemed few and in between
I shouted when others were set free
Though my cupboard was bare, so lean.

Then I heard my precious Lord saying
Because you held on through your storm
Get ready to sound the trumpet, my child
And to set off your deliverance alarm.

Because there's a breakthrough coming,
and it has your name on it
So get ready to receive what's in store
Gear up your mind for your great deliverance
For it's coming your way, and there's more.

No, eyes have not seen, my precious children
Nor ears, nowhere have heard about this
Because only you and I know, He said
What you have sent up on your list.

And it's time for me to move, my soldiers
It's time for your blessing to break forth
No, don't worry about how it's coming
Just continue to look up north.

Because there won't be any doubt when it happens
For your deliverance, it won't be a little bit
Just know, a breakthrough is coming
And it has your name on it.

**SCRIPTURE REFERENCE**
*Psalms 34:17; 107:6*

# You're Next In Line

God it seems like everybody's getting blessed this season
And I'm still in a horrible wreck
I don't mean to bother you my precious Savior
But I must tell you, I am beginning to fret.

For you see, you told me my time was coming
And the blessings falling are also for me
But right now, as I go through my battles dear Savior
Deliverance, I just don't see.

Oh, I hear your prayers my wonderful soldiers
So defeat, I'm here to bind
And to let you know don't fear, and don't you dare give up
Because you're next in line.

Oh, you're next in line my great warriors
No, I didn't forget about you
But I'm setting you up for a mighty deliverance
Oh yes, I'm about to bring you through.

Yes, you're next in line for your blessings
And don't forget I have it all under control
So as you continue to praise my name for your deliverance
Your breakthrough, you will see unfold.

Because you're next in line to receive it
Oh, your victory is an arm length away
So don't let the enemy deceive you any longer
That's why I come to strengthen your hearts today.

Because somebody is ready to step into their blessing
Oh, you can feel it way down in your soul
And if you dare hold on to all I've promised you
It won't be long when you will tell the story not told.

Oh, you should know your time is around the corner
That's why your fight is ever so tough
But before you let the enemy get the best of you
Tell the devil, enough is enough.

For I'm next in line for my miracle
I haven't been holding on this long for naught
So I'm not going to let you take my joy from me
Because my God said my battle is already fought.

Yes, encourage your own self if you have to, this morning
Remembering that I have never lied or failed you
And see yourself walking out of your storm today
And speak it until all things are brand new.

Oh, your deliverance is knocking on your door this morning
Listen and you can hear your breakthrough calling your name
Then continue to lift me up and trust my Word
Believing you are included in this latest rain.

So come on, walk into your victory my loved ones
While shaking off doubt of every kind
For this is the season of breakthroughs, my children
And you're next in line.

### SCRIPTURE REFERENCE
*Psalms 37:1-7; 100:1-5*
*St. John 5:4-9*

# Shake The Devil Up

Sometimes I must bring to remembrance
What I told you I'm going to do
Because in the midst of your waiting, my children
Some are really going through.

I told you this is your time
And the bottom fell out of the floor
Then I told you to step in
And in your face, they slammed the door.

Now my children, my people of God
I hear you saying, enough is enough
So get mad in your spirit today
And shake the devil up.

Yes, shake the devil up
For he thinks you no longer believe
But show him through your praises this day
That all I have promised, you will receive.

And shake the devil up
For he doesn't run this show
Because whatever I said, my children
That's the way things will go.

So shake the devil up
Let him know you're not afraid
But you're stepping up and stepping in
Knowing your way is already made.

Oh, he's been fighting you my children
Trying to take away your joy
Thinking this will make you sit back
Becoming quiet, and ever so coy.

Thinking you'll stop speaking my Word
Because a way, you can't see anymore
But all you're facing, he said
How can you have anything in store?

But shake the devil up
And let him know today
Not even this will stop you
From letting me have my way.

For all of your problems
Just let you know the more
Not only are you getting blessed
But there is much more you have in store.

So don't you dare bow down, my warriors
As though all is lost, is gone
Listen good to me, my children
You, you, and you have a victory song.

Not only are your blessings coming
But something great is about to erupt
So don't just sit there like I'm not talking to you
Come on, shake the devil up.


**SCRIPTURE REFERENCE**
*Psalm 150:1-6*
*St. Matthew 11:12*

## This Is Your Day For A Miracle

You've been holding on my children
Refusing to let go
When the situation caused for you to give up
You stood firm in your spirit, and told defeat, no.

For you knew I was coming through for you
No, you didn't know when
But you knew if you held on long enough
A great deliverance, I would send.

So I come to tell you this day
Now be calm, don't become hysterical
But your wait is over, my wonderful soldiers
For this is your day for a miracle.

Yes, this is your day for a miracle
Your blessings are breaking through
And because you have been holding on despite the odds
You're receiving more than a few.

Oh, this is your day for a miracle
For you've held on long enough
Going through all kinds of misery
Taking all kinds of stuff.

Now this is your day for a miracle
Your day to receive all I promised you
Because you dared to hold on anyway
Despite what you were going through.

Oh, I saw you my precious children
I was there through your every pain
Much taunting and the teasing
And some calling you insane.

They couldn't understand, my precious ones
Why you kept saying you were waiting on me
When everything around you were falling down
And no way, deliverance you could see.

Now this is your day for a miracle
A day for you to rejoice
So you might as well get ready to stand up
And lift me up with a loud voice.

For while you are rejoicing my children
And praising my holy name
Deliverance is going to break forth like you've never known
And you won't, from this day, be the same.

And don't worry about how it's coming
Just continue to look to me
And before you know it, chains will be broken
And from another trial, you'll be free.

So are you ready to receive what's yours today
Whether financial, healing, or spiritual
Oh, whatever you've been believing me for
This is your day for a miracle.

### SCRIPTURE REFERENCE
*St. Matthew 9:20-22; 14:35-36*
*St. John 5:4-9*

## Shout It Out

Somebody is feeling a little discouraged this morning
Because problems seem to be getting out of hand
Somebody wants to throw in the towel today
So get ready my anointed band.

Do you think, my children, I let you get this far
Just to turn you loose
And do you think my loved ones, I'd encourage your hearts
But when you're down, not give you a boost.

Oh, I see the struggles you're facing today
But that only means your battles are nearly fought
So to get you up and on your way again
Get ready to shout it out.

Shout it out, my warriors
Yes, for no devil is going to get you down
For you've come too far and been through too much
To let him get you all tied up and bound.

So shout it out, this morning
All doubt that's trying to fill your minds
So instead of being low in spirit
Satan's tactics, we are about to bind.

So shout it out, every defeated thought
That the enemy plagued you with
Oh, he thought you were coming in torn down this morning
But I will not let you just sit.

For you're too close to give up on me now, my children
And I refuse to let you faint
So no longer do I want to hear those words
Lord it won't happen or God I just can't.

For I'm still your mighty redeemer
And whatever I say, remember it goes
So I've come down just for you this morning
To tell you to shake off all cares and woes.

And get ready to shout it out, my children
For victory is at your door
Yes, you got something to shout about today
For you have so much, my loved ones, in store.

So are you ready my anointed and wonderful band
For it's time to shut the devil down
For after all my children have gone through this season
I won't let their victory not be found.

And are your ready my great and mighty soldiers
Who have held on through it all
Then let's get ready for the last stretch of your trials
Oh, it's time to make a final war call.

Oh yes, satan thought he had you over a barrel
Thinking you'll give in to this drought
But instead, stand to your feet and get ready for release
Come on my children and shout it out.


**SCRIPTURE REFERENCE**
*Ezra 3:11-13*
*Psalms 47:1-3; 98:4*

# I'm Turning It Around

The more you say it's my season, Lord
The worse the trials seem to be
So I need to stop right here, right now
And ask you when will my deliverance, I see?

Because I've been waiting God, and I trust you
But my spirit is getting weary at best
Going from pillar to post, and riding these waves
My soul, my Lord, needs a rest.

Yes, I was getting desperate for a move, my friends
Because I was falling further and further down
Then I heard my Lord say, hold on tight
For my child, I'm turning it around.

I'm turning it around, it's what I'm doing for you
So don't let the enemy cause you to sway
Yes, I'm moving in the spirit, just for you
And as I speak, I'm doing it today.

Yes, I'm turning it around, I'm getting things straight
And soon you will also see
That I didn't leave or forsake you, my child
But what I said will come to be.

I'm turning it around, so don't despair
But keep your eyes on the prize
For it doesn't matter how far down you are
My child, soon you will arise.

I know your situation looks difficult this morning
But remember the blessings you're walking into
So look at these problems for the last time
Because all things will become new.

Yes the enemy, he wants to discourage you
Saying, how long have they said it's your time
They keep telling you to hold on awhile longer
But your victory, you still can't find.

But I'm turning it around, it doesn't matter what he says
Remember, the devil is the master liar
So when he tells you, you're going further and further down
Know that I'm taking you higher.

So continue to look to the hills, my child
Knowing, this too will pass
Yes, then think about all I've done before
And when I brought you out last.

Oh, the devil told you, you wouldn't make it then
But didn't I come through for you
And if I blessed you and helped you before
Be encouraged, again I'll bring you through.

So it's time to put satan where he belongs
Way down under the ground
Yes, make him a liar and give me some praise
And watch me, for I'm turning it around.


**SCRIPTURE REFERENCE**
*Genesis — chapters 37, 39-41*
*Jeremiah 32:27*

## It's Just A Praise Away

God I need to talk to you, I told Him
About a matter that's close to my heart
It's not that I don't trust you, Lord
For you've proven yourself to me from the start.

But you see, they keep telling me my deliverance is nigh me
That it's right at my door
Have faith, I keep hearing from your servants, my Jesus
And I'll experience blessings, I'd never known before.

So why is my world yet crashing down, sweet Savior
When I took to heart every Word you would say
Then I heard my Lord speak ever so gently
Saying my child, it's just a praise away.

He said, it's just a praise away
I heard you, now you listen to me
You've been looking so long with your natural eye
But come with me, so in the spirit you'll see.

For it's just a praise away
Your blessing, it is nigh your door
The answer my child, has been sent to you
But satan is trying to hold up, what's in store.

Oh, but it's just a praise away
No, the devil can't stop my show
So before we go on, you must do this one thing
Stop letting him make you feel so low.

For you see, I've come my precious servant
To let you know, your answer is on its way down
For I knew it would stir up your spirit
And cause you to make a heavenly sound.

And when praises go up, He told me
Then your answer, satan must let go
For he can't stand you glorifying me, my child
When you should be feeling low.

Oh, it's just a praise away
So don't you dare give up on me
For this is not the time to throw in the towel
To let it all go, and to bow.

So let satan know, you know what he's doing
For from the moment you prayed, I moved
Sending the answer you needed, my child
To cause your path to be smoothed.

And every time I sent a servant to lift your spirit
It seemed your problem increasingly got worse
He was just trying to stop you from lifting me up
Then I said Lord, I knew all of this at first.

So I said Lord, I'm not going to dwell on what I used to think
Or how I reacted to my problems, just today
But I'm going to lift you up for bringing me through
For I know, it's just a praise away.

## SCRIPTURE REFERENCE
*Daniel 10:11-13*
*Acts 16:25-26*

## I'm Praising My Way Out Of This Storm

I'm going to try to make it through this rhyme
But I feel a strong yearning down in my soul
Like something great is about to happen, God's people
Like many blessings are about to unfold.

Oh, I've gone through much, God's soldiers
But God said, my time is right now, I'll see
That's why I can't help myself this morning
Because God has never lied to me.

So although I'm trying hard to contain myself
If I break out, don't be alarmed
If you see me pick them up and put them down
I'm just praising my way out of this storm.

Yes, I'm praising my way out of this storm this morning
Because God told me my battle has been fought
He said, I know you've been going through much, my child
But the enemy's tactics, I did halt.

So I'm praising my way out of this storm
Because I see clear skies up ahead
And I'm not worried about what the enemy tried to show me
Because I know what my God has said.

That's why I'm praising my way out of this storm
So if you must, go on with your plans
Because I should have been buried deep down under the ground
If it hadn't been for Jesus holding my hand.

Oh, I can't wait until the battle is over
To give my God His due praise
Because when I look over my life
I see Him blessing me in so many ways.

One time when I thought I was drowning
Another time when the flames seemed, oh so hot
No matter how disastrous the situations were
Destroy me, the enemy could not.

That's why I'm praising my way out of this storm today
Because just like before, there is a brighter day ahead
Because after I've done all I could do
My God took over, yes He led.

So I'm lifting up my God on this morning
And no devil, anywhere, will stop me
For I refuse to give up in this battle
And stop God from making me free.

So who has the enemy been fighting in their storm
Tossing you to and fro
Trying to make you give it all up
Making you believe your deliverance is not so.

Then come on, let's make the devil out of a liar
We refuse to sit here acting all tired and worn
So because we know God's got our backs
We're praising our way out of these storms.


**SCRIPTURE REFERENCE**
*Psalm 150:1-6*
*Acts 16:25-26*

## Expect The Unexpected

I was giving glory to my most precious God
For all He was about to do
For delivering me and bringing me up
I was thanking Him for taking me through.

Then when I heard the Lord speak to my spirit
I couldn't contain myself anymore
For I knew without a shadow of doubt, my dear friends
That I was walking through some mighty doors.

But my Savior, He didn't stop there, oh no
Then I no longer saw my life as being hectic
For my God whispered these words to me
And said, my child, expect the unexpected.

Oh, expect the unexpected
Then He said, tell my people today
To hold on, and don't let go
For help is on the way.

And to expect the unexpected
For you're getting double for all you've been through
Oh, satan thought he was counting you out
But he doesn't know what he did for you.

So start to expect the unexpected, He kept saying
For you're about to walk into something great
Oh yes, be encouraged, for it's yours for the taking
And don't worry, I will not be at all, late.

So are you ready God's great people today
To step up and step out in our Lord
Praising Him as you watch Him move
Being determined to be on one accord.

Because God said, this is truly your year, my great warriors
So get ready to take it, and if you have to, by force
No, don't let anything or anyone stop you
Or cause you to go off course.

And expect the unexpected this season
For you have waited long enough
Receiving many bumps and bruises from the enemy
Standing strong even when times were rough.

So now it's time to worship our loving Savior
Praising Him as we near the end of our storms
Knowing, no matter what satan threw at us
He still could do us no harm.

So come on great people of God, this morning
Let's let God know, yes we believe
Every Word He's saying about bringing us up
Lord this morning, we do receive.

So we make no excuses for our behavior
For this Word in our hearts, have been greatly affected
For our God is not only about to bring us out
But He told us to expect the unexpected.

## SCRIPTURE REFERENCE
*Genesis 50:18-20*
*2 Chronicles 1:6-12*
*Joel 2:21-26*

## There's A Blessing Coming Your Way

Oh yes, the devil thought he had you good, didn't he
Why even go today, he said
Look, this must be a sign from heaven
You know you need the rest, so go back to bed.

Struggling to get here this morning
One thing happening after the next
I'm trying to get there Jesus, you said
But what's the use, my spirit is all so vexed.

But then God put a go ahead down in my spirit
Dear friends, let me tell you why today
For He said, if you can just make it through these doors
There's a blessing coming your way.

Yes, there's a blessing coming your way
That's why there has been such a fight
For the devil knows, God's great people
How close you are to seeing the light.

For there's a blessings coming your way
Yes, you made it just in time
That's why everything was going wrong this morning
Even your shoes or keys, you couldn't find.

Because there's a blessing coming your way
No, the devil can't stop it now
Oh, he tried to discourage your hearts and spirits
And try to make some of you stop and bow.

But praise God, you made it
You said, no devil is going to stop God's show
You made up your minds to get here anyway
No matter how bad you felt, or how low.

And God said, because of your perseverance, dear ones
Just watch me move for you
No, eyes have not seen, nor ears heard
What all I'm about to do.

For there's a blessing coming your way
I know what people have said
But you can let them know, I'm still with you
And guess what, you are still the head.

So God said, hold your head up my dear children
For you made it through these doors
Yes, I know you asked me to help you
But I'm going to do that, and more.

Yes, gear yourself up and get ready
For what I'm going to do for you today
Oh, the battle was heated, but you made it
Now, there's a blessing coming your way.

## SCRIPTURE REFERENCE
*Deuteronomy 28:3-8*
*Isaiah 64:4*
*1 Corinthians 2:9*

## There's A Story Behind My Praise

What's wrong with these people, you hear some say
They're always jumping around
Lifting their hands, they said to their Jesus
Falling all over the ground.

I wish they would tell me why they're doing this
Why they break out and run
Why they begin to shout hallelujah
Before an explanation is even done.

Well my friends, you may not be able to tell it all
For God has blessed you in so many ways
So to sum it all up, when they ask you why
Tell them, there's a story behind my praise.

Yes, there's a story behind my praise
Oh, I wish I could tell you more
But I only need to think about the goodness of my Jesus
And I'm up again on the floor.

Because there's a story behind my praise
Oh, God has been so good to me
He's been opening doors and making a way
And yes, He has made my soul free.

Oh, there's a story behind my praise
So pardon me if you will
But if you knew half of what God has done for me
You wouldn't be able yourself, to sit still.

Yes, I'm trying to contain myself this morning
But thinking about Him makes me want to shout
No, you weren't there when He came through for me
You don't know the many battles my God has fought.

That's why I better stop talking about my Jesus
Because I'm trying very hard to be good
I want to sit very calmly and tell the story
About how He brought me over, if I could.

But you see, there's a story behind my praise
Is all I have the time to say
Before I can't help myself once again
Letting go, and letting God have His way.

Oh yes, I'm still going through this morning
And it looks like I won't win
But as always, before I fall, He picks me up
And once again, my Savior, my God defends.

So I know even with what I'm going through this morning
Oh no, don't feel sorry for me
For I know my God, He will bring me out
A brighter day is about to be.

Then here I go again, jumping up in my Jesus
Running around or standing with my hands raised
And just in case I won't be able to explain it all
Just know, there's a story behind my praise.

## SCRIPTURE REFERENCE
*2 Samuel 6:11-22*

# I'm Alright Now

Sometimes your situations, your problems, your cares
Can get the best of you
For you do all you know to do, my friends
And you find yourself still going through.

But before I could let go of God's promises
I went to Him in prayer
And said, God, but you told me to look to you
For all my problems, you do bear.

And let me tell you, He did come through for me
So what you may see from now on may raise an eyebrow
For I was as low as low can get
But I'm alright now.

Yes, I'm alright now
But to tell you, how do I begin
For when it felt like I couldn't take another step
God's mighty deliverance grace, He did send.

So I'm alright now
For it looked like I was going under fast
But my great and mighty Savior
Gave me the strength I needed to last.

Oh, I'm alright now
And I'm ready to fight once more
With my Jesus by my side
I'll receive all I have in store.

No, this story has no sad ending
That's why I must give my Lord some praise
And what I love about my Lord and Savior
He's not just taking me through a phase.

For He's here with me for the long haul
To give me everything I need
He told me, as long as I stay in His precious will
My spirit, He'll continue to feed.

Oh, I'm alright now
For the devil thought he had me down for the count
But what my Lord has put down in me
I'm able to rise up and mount.

And I'm not going to stop here either
For God has greater plans for me
He said, what I have for you my child today
No eyes, anywhere can see.

So you keep reaching and obeying, He said
And don't settle for anything less
For what I have in store for you
I can sum up, as being better than the best.

So where satan thought he had me
Was strong enough to make a strong saint bow
But my God, He came through like a mighty wind
And I'm alright now.


## SCRIPTURE REFERENCE
*Psalms 18:32-34; 107:28-30; 121:1-3*

# It's Not Over Until God Says It's Over

I know it looks like it's the end of your trial
The final curtain has been closed
All that know your situation, tell you
Your defeat my friend, only God knows.

But as you get ready to pick up your shattered pieces
And move on in this precious walk you're in
You hear a voice from heaven strong and clear
With a message just for you, He sends.

You hear, I know it looks like this battle, you have lost
And because of your love for me, you try to be calm and sober
But I have a Word for you
that has come straight from the Lord
It's not over until God says it's over.

Oh, it's not over until God says it's over
And God said to tell you, it's not over yet
I know you have been knocked down, pushed down, and turned
upside down
But God said your victory is still set.

No, it's not over until God says it's over
So get ready for round four
For this time is the clincher, He said
You're about to open your door.

Oh, it's not over until God says it's over
So new strength He must impart in you
Oh, I know you want to move on and
say I gave it my best shot
But God said, I'm here to help bring you on through.

Oh yes, He said, the difference with my great warriors
They don't give up because it seems their battles are lost
For they remember in the natural how badly it looked
As Jesus hung on the cross.

For three days He laid in His grave
And the disciples thought, what do we do now
But Jesus taught them on that third day
If God said it, never give up or bow.

And they saw it wasn't over until God says it's over
And today He's speaking to someone here too
But God, you're saying, what do I do about this situation
Do I move forward, or stand still, I don't have a clue.

But God said it's still yours for the taking
So continue to stand on His Word
And though you can't see your victory at all
By faith, you must hold on to all you've heard.

Yes, somebody was feeling a little weary today
So God said, I've come just for you
For you've fought too long in this battle
Just to give up and say Lord, I'm through.

So get ready to be recharged on this morning
And after today you won't be laid back or sober
Because God is going to put His fight back in you
Because it's not over until God says it's over.

## SCRIPTURE REFERENCE
*St. Mark 15:22-47; 6:1-6*
*St. John 11:1-44*

# But God

Oh, the enemy thought he had me good, my friends
I'm telling you, I was down for the count
Because my problems, they kept piling up
Yes, much tension in me, began to mount.

Oh, it was coming to a point in Jesus
Where I felt, Lord I can't take anymore
Even though you keep telling me, my precious Savior
Hold on, for you have much more in store.

Then when it seemed like it was over this time
On this journey, I could no longer trod
Oh, I'm telling you good people today
I was on my way out, but God.

But God, came through like a whirlwind
Saying, my child, I'll never fail you
And it's time for satan to let go now
And let old things become brand new.

But God, He didn't leave me, no He didn't
Yes, He came through right on time
And though I was feeling all bound up inside
The enemy, he began to bind.

But God, when satan said, you lost this one
God wiped all my tears away
And gave me some news from heaven
Now listen to what I say.

Then He said, gird yourself up this morning
No, my way, don't you dare let go
But think on the goodness of my Word on today
For it's time out for you feeling low.

For I am still your way maker, my child
It doesn't matter what comes your way
Oh, I told you over and again, I'll bless you
And guess what, this is your day.

But God, is all I can say this morning
For blessing me once again
For pulling me out when I was drowning
Causing me to walk on dry land.

Oh, I must give my Lord much praise this morning
For He always knows what to do
When there was no way for deliverance this time
Yes, my Lord, He brought me through.

So I magnify Him, my redeemer
I thank Him for not letting me down
Oh, I worship my Lord this day, my friends
No way I can wear a frown.

So when you see me still yet rejoicing
On this journey that we trod
It's because it was all sewn up, it was over for me
I was down for the count, but God.

## SCRIPTURE REFERENCE
*Daniel 6:4-25*
*St. Luke 13:11-13*
*Acts 12:1-11*

## You Just Have To Let Go

You know it's good to be well-mannered
Every hair on your head in place
Not bringing attention to yourself
It doesn't matter what you face.

But then there are times when you reminisce
On just how great God is, how good
Just blessing you and continually keeping you
Even though you haven't been all you should.

Oh, you don't plan on doing it
You think, today I'll just lay low
But something way down in you won't let it be
And you realize you just have to let go.

You just have to let go
And let God's spirit take control
Saying, anything you want to do with me
Here I am God, make and mold.

Yes, you just have to let go
Because His love won't let you rest
Knowing you're on the winners side with Jesus
You're with the best of the best.

And you just have to let go
You're thinking, I don't mean to offend
But God keeps showing me in the spirit
A great release, He's about to send.

Yes, there's a time and place for everything
But oh, hallelujah keeps bubbling up
And you say, Lord I better do something about this thing
For I feel an overflowing in my cup.

I'm trying to sit still, Jesus
I'm trying to maintain composure in here
But it will take just one more, glory to God
And I'm gone Lord, I fear.

Yes, you just have to let go
So you say neighbor, pardon me a little bit
I don't mean to be rude today
But I'm about to have a Holy Ghost fit.

I know I won't be able to finish telling you
Why I must do what I'm about to do
But let me tell you, you'll be right there with me
If you knew all He's brought me through.

Then you'll say, here I am Jesus
You've done too much for me to sit down
It's because of you I'm free today
No longer am I bound.

So you'll say, excuse me good people
I tried to move with the flow
But I've been thinking about the goodness of Jesus
Then you just have to let go.

### SCRIPTURE REFERENCE
*2 Samuel 6:14-21*
*Psalm 103:1-22*

## That Was Then, But This Is Now

I woke up on this morning
Ready in my God to fight
I could sense it way down in my spirit, yeah
I am going up to higher heights.

If I talk about then, great people of God
It's just to let you know where I'm going
Oh, take a good look at me now
Because pretty soon, this child of God will be soaring.

For yes, I've had some mighty huge struggles, my friends today
Enough to make a person want to bow
But I'm ready to stand up and let the devil know
Oh, that was then, but this is now.

Yes, that was then, but this is now
No, the enemy can't get me like he did in times past
Because I'm rededicating my life back to Jesus
I'm going to consecrate my life, pray, and fast.

For you see that was then, but this is now
You won't see me crying over spilled milk
But I'm going to wipe it up, for I got greater things in store
More salvation, Holy Ghost, pearls, even silk.

So that was then, but this is now
My attitude, God surely did change
The whole way of seeing how God works
Yes, my Lord, He did rearrange.

For let me tell you,
this past year brought much heartache and trauma
Yes, my heart was truly crushed
So much disappointments and let downs, people of God
That it just didn't seem just.

Then in the midst of all my misery
Other whammies, the enemy yet snuck in
All kinds of problems, yes he did
The enemy, against me, he'd send.

But guess what, that was then, but this is now
Because I got my head on straight
So satan should have gotten me when I was down and out
Because here comes a news flash now, it's a little too late.

Because God knows how to heal a broken spirit
And He knows how to lift up a bowed down head
Yes, God knows how to open sealed doors too
Just like His precious Word said.

So when satan tried his tricks on this morning
He didn't know what God had done
He put a get up and go, back down in my feet
And said, my child, it's time for you to get up and run.

So when satan said,
oh you know you're not feeling up to it this morning
Stay home, they won't miss you anyhow
I thought, that might have worked in times past
Yes, that was then, but this is now.

### SCRIPTURE REFERENCE
*Judges 16: 1-21; 23-30*
*St. Matthew 26:69-75*
*Acts 2: 11-40; 3: 1-8*

# I'm Going To Keep On Keeping On

It's an exuberating morning
Oh, it just makes you want to shout
Yes, I know satan has been trying to stop you
Asking, what are you rejoicing about?

Your life is still in an uproar
Your world is crumbling down
And there you are still jumping around
Even though victory can't be found.

Well, I'm going to make you mad, satan
For I'm still going to praise my Lord
Yes, I'm going to keep on keeping on
No, praising Him won't be hard.

Yes, I'm going to keep on keeping on
I'm going to give God my best
For He's been much too good to me
For me to give Him anything less.

I'm going to keep on keeping on
Because heaven is my goal
So keep on shaping me, my Savior
Make me into your perfect mold.

Yes, I'm going to keep on keeping on
This little pain can't make me cease
It only draws me closer to God
Makes my love for Him increase.

Just you trying to stop me satan
Lets me know I'm on the right track
So I'm going to keep on praising my God
No matter how you act.

So once again, this is a beautiful morning
Lord, a good day to lift you up
And since there are so many things coming against me
I can use an extra filling in my cup.

Because I'm going to keep on keeping on
For I know God, you're on my case
And I know every praise I give to you
Will never go to waste.

So I'm sorry for any delay, you all
But I must prove the devil wrong
Come telling me this morning
That I don't have a victory song.

But I know it's not in the feeling
Or how my situation looks
It's all about my precious Jesus
And I got to tell you, on Him I'm hooked.

So it doesn't matter what you try to do satan
I'm still going to blow God's horn
And continue to praise my Savior
As I keep on keeping on.

## SCRIPTURE REFERENCE
*Psalm 150:1-6*
*Philippians 4:4-6*

# God Is Too Good

Just thinking about the goodness of you, Jesus
My bright and morning star
My soul must shout hallelujah
For being the wonderful Savior you are.

For you are the lily of my valley
You are my one, my all and all
You never, ever let me down
On you, I can always call.

Just trying to think of a few words
To describe you, if I could
Nothing can come closer Lord
Than God is too good.

Oh, God is too good
For He's my hope when all is lost
He comes through in the nick of time
And shows the world He's still boss.

Yes, God is too good
For He's my joy when there is none
When I feel like I can't make it
He gives me strength to run.

My God is too good
Oh, I'm more than a conqueror through Him
With Christ, nothing is impossible
Nor victory is ever too slim.

Oh, He is my redeemer
My peace in the midst of a storm
My great and mighty protector
He lets nothing do me real harm.

So when I think about all He's brought me through
The many mountains, He has moved
When I think about how He's brought me up
And the crooked places, He's made smooth.

I must say God is too good
No, no one can compare
To His wonderful grace and mercy
To His tender loving care.

Oh, it makes me want to stop right now
And give my God some praise
For the many times He has kept me
I can't even count the ways.

But Lord, I say thank you
With my hands lifted high today
And I bless you on this morning
So sweet Jesus have your way.

No, I can't look as if my own action
Has been as the Word says it should
But I must praise my Lord today
Because God is too good.

### SCRIPTURE REFERENCE
*Exodus 13:1-22; 14:1-31*
*Isaiah 9:6-7*
*Zephaniah 3:17*
*Philippians 4:19*
*Hebrews 13:6*

## You Owe Me Some Praise

I was awakened early this glorious morning
Out of a deep and sound sleep
And I could tell by the urgency in His voice
That what the Lord wanted, couldn't keep.

So I stumbled out of bed, still drowsy
But anxious to get before the Lord
Beginning to pray in the spirit
That our souls could be on one accord.

Oh, it didn't take long before He answered
Bringing my room up in a blaze
For He said, my child I come to tell you
You owe me some praise.

You owe me some praise, He said again
For all I've done for you this day
For if it wasn't for me being with you
In this trial, you couldn't stay.

So you owe me some praise
And it must come from the bottom of your heart
Because nobody but me has been with you
Yes, I've seen you through from the start.

You owe me some praise, yes you do
And I've come to collect my dues
For I've come every time you called me, my child
Keeping satan from harming you.

Just think about it, my wonderful soldier
How things could have gone this week
But I intervened just for you
When the enemy against you tried to speak.

I wouldn't let him get the best of you
And warned you before he got too close
I know it looked like you were losing the battle
But he can't stand against my great host.

Yes, you owe me some praise
I know the trials have been coming left and right
But when you stop and think about it, my child
You are indeed winning the fight.

For you are always one step before the enemy
Because I show you what he's trying to do
And when he huffs and puffs to blow your blessings away
I build up a wall to protect you.

But you think these trials are too much for you
Oh, I heard your cry, that's why I came
To refocus you, and get you back on track
That you may receive the latter rain.

For didn't you say, to go up in me
A great price, a person pays
Well, I see you coming up my way
So don't just sit there, you owe me some praise.


## SCRIPTURE REFERENCE
*Exodus 15:1-13; 20-21*
*Psalm 86:12-13*

## Don't Tell Me God Is Not Good

Oh, I feel it way down in my spirit
That my God is about to move
All the crooked roads I've been traveling on
My Lord is about to make them smooth.

Yes, whenever I'm at the end of my rope
God won't just let me hang
So I know He's going to pull me up, and bring me over
And take me out with a bang.

That's why with all I'm facing today
I'm not acting the way the devil thinks I should
Because I'm giving God all of me
No, don't tell me God is not good.

Don't tell me God is not good
For it doesn't matter the situation I'm in
Before the enemy can throw his last punch
My Savior comes through and defends.

So don't tell me God is not good
Oh, I know He's going to bring me out
For there has never been a defeat when it comes to my Savior
No, He's never lost any battle He's fought.

So no, don't tell me God is not good
That's why somebody needs to put satan under their feet
For God said, this is not the time to give up on Him
Because you're feeling a little heat.

Oh I know, we have stories to tell today
So don't get us started or we all will cry
But we're not going to let the enemy drag us down
So we're going to praise God until all eyes are dry.

Because we know when it comes down to our Savior
He has a plan for you and me
To bring us through our storm and rain
To deliver us and make us free.

So don't tell me God is not good
No, not even these trials will make us doubt
For we've been in too many battles with Him
He's delivered us in too many bouts.

So we're going to lift God up this morning
Thanking Him for what He's about to do
For we know without a shadow of doubt
That our God is going to see us through.

So if you're feeling a little low in your spirit
Get up and shake the devil off
No, you're not going to sit here and die today
Because we're going to run weariness out of God's house.

And before you know it, you'll be standing up in Jesus
Saying, God did it like no one else could
Yes, when all was lost, He came through just for me
So don't tell me God is not good.

## SCRIPTURE REFERENCE
*2 Kings 4:1-7*
*Psalms 37:25; 100:1-5*
*St. Luke 3:5*

# I Got This

God, this has gone far enough, I told Him one day
Lord, I'm tired of all this pain
When are you going to deliver me, dear Jesus
For I'm drowning in all this rain.

Oh, sometimes I felt I was at the end of my rope
And just couldn't take anymore
Lord, I'd say, I'm not going to make it
If you soon, don't open my door.

Then I heard the Lord's voice softly speaking
And in such a way, His answer I couldn't miss
Soothingly calming my heart and nerves
And saying my child, I got this.

Yes, I got this, my precious warrior
So believe me when I say
This is truly your time and your chance
And deliverance is on the way.

Oh, I got this, He continued to minister
Because I was down so low, I couldn't see
Then He said, get up and praise me, my precious child
For your blessings, that are about to be.

Because I got this, my soldier
So let me do what I do best
Keep on believing me for your every deliverance
And don't settle for anything less.

Oh, sometimes no matter how strong you are
Your problems can weigh you down
Making it hard to hold on to all God says
As you feel yourself about to drown.

But I thank God for being who He is
Who won't let you go out like that
Yes, He knows how to soothe your aching soul
By meeting you where you're at.

Oh I got this, He reassures your heart
As He raises you back up in Him
Making you ready to fight in this battle again
No matter how tough, or victory so slim.

That's why God is here, to minister to someone
Who is feeling low at heart
Giving you what you need in Him
Restoring your strength as from the start.

So let's stand on this morning and shake off all doubt
Because we do win, yes we do
Let's look at our burdens one more time
And say God, I give all of this to you.

And come on God's people, let's get ready to praise Him
Oh, it's time to reach heavenly bliss
For that problem that was getting the best of you
God said don't worry, I got this.


## SCRIPTURE REFERENCE
*Joshua 1:9*
*Proverbs 19:21*
*Isaiah 45:6-7; 55:8-13*
*Romans 8:28*
*1 Corinthians 10:13*

## Just Give Me My Praise

This is your time, my children
So you might as well rejoice
Don't let what you're going through this morning
Stop you from lifting up your voice.

Because I have it all under control, believe me
When I say it's yours, it's now
Refuse to allow satan to discourage you
Or cause you, in this trial, to bow.

Just think about all the doors I'm opening
Oh, your blessings are coming in so many ways
All I need you to do for me
Is just give me my praise.

Just give me my praise, my children
For bringing you up and out
Oh, I know the devil is trying to fool you
But I am right now fighting your bout.

So just give me my praise, my children
Show me you still yet believe
By continuing to bless my name
And watch the deliverance, you receive.

Just give me my praise, my soldiers
That's all I need you to do
Don't wait until your battle is over
But shout your way all the way through.

Oh, the devil, he has been trying to make you think
That I wasn't talking to you
Yes, I am a deliverer, He said
But no way am I bringing you through.

But the devil is a liar, I'm here to tell you
It's yours for the taking for sure
For I've seen you holding on to all you've heard
I've seen the suffering you've endured.

So just give me my praise, my warriors
Are you ready to shout for joy
For I'm going to do all I said to you
So this is no time to be coy.

But let's stomp all over the devil this morning
Refusing, in this trial, to doubt
But believing me with all that is within you
That your battle is already fought.

Oh, if you could only see what I see
How your walls are falling down flat
How very close you are to your deliverance
You'll do more than a mere pitty pat.

Because I'm coming through like a mighty whirlwind
And your haters, they will be amazed
And all you need to do to show me your thanks
Is just give me my praise.

## SCRIPTURE REFERENCE
*Joshua 6:20*
*1 Chronicles 16:8*
*Psalms 42:11; 71:14; 106:1; 138:1*
*Acts 16:16-40*

## You Ain't Seen Nothing Yet

I don't' mean to offend the English major
Who works hard to use the proper words
But you know, I got to tell what God told me
And I have to say exactly what I heard.

As I was listening to the Lord speak, good people
And as I saw the mighty move of my Lord
I began to feel many weights fall off of me
No, my troubles no longer seemed as hard.

Yes, I was ready to run on some more in my Jesus
For I knew my deliverance in God was set
But I couldn't be content about what He had done
When I heard, but you ain't seen nothing yet.

Oh, you ain't seen nothing yet, God's mighty warriors
So don't get comfortable because of what happened before
Because God said,
there are mountains yet to be moved in your life
No, He has not opened your every door.

Oh, you ain't seen nothing yet
Oh yes, your God, He blessed your souls
But go with Him a little higher, He said
And you'll have a story that, by you, could only be told.

For you ain't seen nothing yet
Oh yes, and He's talking about you too
Because you're saying Lord, it can't be me
With all I've been going through.

Because we can go through so long, God's people
That we can begin to think that's where we must belong
But God said you only need the faith of a mustard seed
So you too, have a victory song.

And because God has moved so mightily in your life
You thought it couldn't get any better than this
But God said, He adjure you on this week
Not one time with Him, you should miss.

Because you ain't seen nothing yet
God said, you only touched the surface, you'll see
Because eyes sure enough, haven't seen thus far
What, in your life, is about to be.

So if I were you, I'd shake off every doubt I have left
That's trying to hang on to the very end
For God said He didn't forget about His precious ones
And yes, you are worthy for all that He's about to send.

So stand to your feet, why don't you
And let's get ready to shout for joy
Knowing that God was there even in your lowest hour
Don't you dare start acting all quiet and coy.

But get ready to receive some more blessings, great people
Because your time and chance has finally met
And God said,
when you thought it couldn't get any better for you
You ain't seen nothing yet.

## SCRIPTURE REFERENCE
*Deuteronomy 28:12*
*Isaiah 64:4*
*1 Corinthians 2:9*
*2 Corinthians 9:8*
*Ephesians 3:20-21*

## <u>You're Closer Than You Think</u>

I'm going through too much, I hear you
The Lord is saying today
One thing after another
When is it going to let up, you say.

You keep telling me, it's my time
But I find myself going deeper in the hole
When am I going to tell the story
You say, still is not yet told.

But contrary to the way it looks, my children
I want you to know, you won't sink
So hold on, no don't let go
Because you're closer than you think.

Yes, you're closer than you think
To receive all I promised you
Neither be weary in your well doing
For I am going to bring you through.

For you're closer than you think
That's why you're being fought so
So when the devil tells you to give it all up
In your spirit, tell him no.

For you're closer than you think
And you've come too far to quit now
So don't let the enemy take your praise
Or make you bend or bow.

Just think about how long you've been waiting
Refusing to let go of my Word
It didn't matter what others said or did
You didn't back off from what you heard.

But you continued in me during your rough time
Even when you wanted to let go
You found new strength to continue on
Yes, you refused to stay down low.

So now you're closer than you think
This is not the time to give up
When I'm getting ready to move for you
When your blessings are about to erupt.

Just remember in times past
When it looked like I wouldn't come through
But didn't I show up, my children
And I came through just for you.

And now, if I could show you in the spirit
Just how close you are to being set free
You'd be up right now, shouting for joy
If you could only see what I see.

So this morning shake off what satan is trying to do
And from praise and joy, continue to drink
For deliverance is coming your way, my children
And you're closer than you think.


**SCRIPTURE REFERENCE**
*2 Kings 6:15-17*
*Isaiah 40:31; 65:24*
*Galatians 6:9*
*Hebrews 6:15*

## Keep Your Praise Up

Oh, I'm coming through like I told you
And my children, it won't be too long
Delivering you where you need it most
Righting your every wrong.

I know the enemy wants to make some of you think
That this season is not meant for you
But when I spoke, your time has finally come
My loved ones, you were included in that number too.

So hold on to all I told you
For your breakthrough is about to erupt
And all I need you to do right now
Is to keep your praise up.

Oh, keep your praise up, my loved ones
For it's music to my ears
And as you continue to lift me up and worship me
I'll comfort and cast down all your fears.

So keep your praise up
Because it's breaking down your every wall
And no, don't start worrying about what you see now
For no way I will let you fall.

But keep your praise up
Let me continue to hear from you
Then watch me turn your situation around
Making all things in your life brand new.

I know you keep hearing me say it
But my children, believe what I say
Because eyes have not yet seen, my warriors
The help that's on its way.

For you've been waiting patiently for my deliverance
You've been shaking off your every doubt
When times grew hard, and you saw no way out
You reminisce on all the battles I fought.

So I'm here to tell you to keep your praise up
Don't let the enemy stop your flow
Don't let him discourage your hearts
Telling you I'm moving a little too slow.

For you know I'm going to bring you out
Open your eyes, don't you see me moving now
So shake yourself off if you're weary
For this is no time for you to bow.

Because you have blessings coming your way
And no devil can stop what's yours
And don't worry about how I'm going to do it
For I'm getting ready to unlock all your doors.

So are you ready, great children of mine
To let me fill your every cup
Then don't just sit like I'm not talking to you
Come on, keep your praise up.

## SCRIPTURE REFERENCE
*2 Samuel 22:47-50*
*2 Kings 6:15-17*
*Psalm 95:1-2*
*1 Thessalonians 5: 16-18*
*Philippians 4:6*
*Hebrews 13:15*

*Deborah L. Hayman*

*Words of Inspiration Ministries*
*P O Box 38432*
*St. Louis, MO  63138*

www.ingramcontent.com/pod-product-compliance
Lightning Source LLC
Chambersburg PA
CBHW060157070426
42447CB00033B/2195